Scott Joplin: The Life and Legacy of the King of Ragtime

By Charles River Editors

About Charles River Editors

Charles River Editors provides superior editing and original writing services across the digital publishing industry, with the expertise to create digital content for publishers across a vast range of subject matter. In addition to providing original digital content for third party publishers, we also republish civilization's greatest literary works, bringing them to new generations of readers via ebooks.

Sign up here to receive updates about free books as we publish them, and visit Our Kindle Author Page to browse today's free promotions and our most recently published Kindle titles.

Introduction

"What is scurrilously called ragtime is an invention that is here to stay. That is now conceded by all classes of musicians." – Scott Joplin

Aspiring professional musicians have in every country and in every genre faced long odds. In the classical music market, the rarified air of public success makes room for only a few, and to even create a sustainable income for most is problematic. For the African American classical musician of the 19th century, the difficulties ran far deeper than the profession's inherent obstacles. In the post-Civil

War period, the first task for an African American artist was to prove to the presiding white society that he or she possessed the intelligence to pursue creative fields, talent aside. The image of the subservient field worker embedded in the white American imagination largely overruled the sight of a black man or woman performing mainstream works composed by the great European composers.

In the world of composition, artists commonly bring their cultural origins and familiar forms of expression into the process as a central feature of their work. In America, this presented an additional barrier to the 19th century African Americans who relied upon a largely oral music and dance tradition from a continent already receiving scant respect for European-style achievements. Even for the white American musicians, European bias had always inferred that the prevailing masterpieces could only come from a German, French, Italian, Spanish or Russian composer, not a black man from a backwoods former colony. Thus, for African Americans, such a prejudice was nearly insurmountable. Perhaps the greatest feat of all was to convince an elite concertgoing public that mixing European and African musical features merited at the least respectability, and at the most a sense of appreciation. To the white tie audience, those African forms included dance maneuvers honed and enjoyed in fields and alleyways. Many musical techniques for accompanying these forms were developed on the banjo and other folk instruments, unthinkable for an invitation to the concert hall.

Despite a general dearth of African American names rising to musical prominence during the years of Reconstruction, black talent existed in good measure for both popular and classical genres, and among the most notable musicians celebrated in the present day is composer Scott Joplin, who in his day earned the moniker "King of Ragtime."[1] Joplin's use of ragtime as a piano genre was as natural to African American dances as the waltz was to Europeans. The new African-based musical language grew to such popularity that piano rags were programmed on formal classical programs. Originally employed as a verb, as in to "rag" a rhythm, the genre was first referred to as the "jig-piano"[2] style. Ragtime features off-beat rhythms, a heavily accented first beat with the left hand making fast leaps to include the harmony. Pieces of the genre are as visually distinctive as they are in sound. Popular with honky-tonk pianists working along the Mississippi and Missouri Rivers, ragtime became the "predominant style of American popular music"[3] by the end of the 19th century. Dance steps like the cakewalk,

[1] Encyclopaedia Britannica, Ragtime – www.britannica.com/art/ragtime#ref279958

[2] TSHA, Texas State Historical Association, Texas Handbook, Joplin, Scott – www.tsaonline.org/handbook/online/articles/fjo70

[3] Encyclopaedia Britannica

inspired by minstrel shows featuring modes of black banjo playing, were unlikely to be incorporated into white dance for many years to come, but white musicians incorporated the sound into their own daily repertoires as a pleasing style of melody and rhythm. The days of minstrel performances, in which white performers costumed themselves in black face without societal backlash, were eventually replaced by black performers such as Joplin and others like him. Once free from such mockery, black artists were free to produce musical offerings from the authentic culture. The term "rag," according to Joplin's use of the term, represented a musical evolution, an abrupt, edgy approach to the musical phrase, suggesting a "ragged movement."[4]

Mixing his gifts for ragtime, a forerunner of American jazz, with a classical education, Joplin produced hundreds of short piano works based on African vocal and dance music, and he worked tirelessly to bring them to a state of validation in the white American and European music world. Moving beyond miniatures, Joplin ventured into the bastion of European opera, highlighting blacks' intent to elevate and modernize black culture through education in the process. Paralleling the aspirations of Booker T. Washington, W.E.B. Du Bois, and Marcus Garvey, Joplin is often viewed as an influential part of a rising black

---

[4] AZ Quotes, Scott Joplin – www.azquotes.com/author/42237_Scott_Joplin

society, excelling in an alien environment full of inequality. He shared fame among the top ragtime players in the nation along with artists such as Louis Chauvin and Thomas M. Turpin, the father of St. Louis ragtime, as well as Tony Jackson in New Orleans. While many ragtime artists were less concerned about incorporating the genre into the classical world, Joplin considered it to be a branch of formal music and fought for its recognition as such. Acceptance by the classical world signified a long-term validation for his new genre, and he was willing to suffer decades of rejection to witness the breakthrough.

Scott Joplin: The Life and Legacy of the King of Ragtime profiles how he became one of 20th century music's most influential figures. Along with pictures of important people, places, and events, you will learn about Scott Joplin like never before.

Southern Roots

The precise date and location of Joplin's birth remain unknown, but the time frame is generally set between June 1867 and January 1868, with various locations along the Texas and Arkansas border claiming to be the site. November 24, 1868 was for a time thought to be Joplin's likely birthdate, but research undertaken by biographer Ed Berlin has cast much doubt on the earlier consensus.

It is generally agreed that he was raised in the region of Texarkana. Communities along the border of northeast Texas were predominantly white in the western districts. His residence was likely poor, African American, and segregated, which likely places his origins closer to the Arkansas side. The Texas State Historical Association appears firm in its belief that Joplin's birthplace is Cavern Spring, near Linden, but even if so, Joplin's family did not stay in Texas long before gravitating to the eastern side of Texarkana. Census records place him there by the time he was two-years-old, but some family movement obscured the original data.

Joplin's mother, Florence Givens, sustained the family as a caretaker of the church, cleaning homes and working as a laundress. Many of her white clients possessed pianos. One among them, attorney W.H. Cook, offered Given's son access to the family instrument while she worked. His father, Giles Joplin, had gained his freedom only a few years before his son's birth, and he took up work as a railroad laborer.

Both parents possessed musical backgrounds. Florence was a locally notable singer and banjo player while Giles was a somewhat adept violinist, and as a former slave, his acquisition of such skills and access to knowledge of European classical music was uncommon. At an early age, Scott was coached on European forms and styles, but the musical relationship between father and son was not to last. Believing that music was no suitable profession for any black American, he pushed his son to join him on the railroad at the earliest age possible, an effort Florence roundly resisted. Giles left the family early in the children's lives and took another wife, leaving a nearly unsurmountable burden on Florence. Scott's siblings included Monroe, Myrtle, Ossie, Robert, and William, all of whom grew up with their mother. All the children studied violin to one degree or another, and from a young Scott added the cornet to his list of interests.

Giles' second marriage failed as well, after which he moved in with his older son, Monroe. In later years, his health failed to the point where his only employment consisted of community gardening, and he was forced to stop working when his legs at last became useless. The railroad versus music as a career would be an ongoing argument between Giles and Florence until his death. For the elder Joplin and many of the freed slaves, the post-war destruction and wave of new legal constraints promoted a belief that a black man lived in the South "without meaning and purpose."[5] The emancipated slave was in his various conditions both happy and confused, legally freed from bondage but enslaved to Jim Crow as a means of preserving the old order.

Florence Given's influence on her son steered him toward the church, where he acquired great familiarity with American spiritual forms of music. Church was not reserved for Sunday alone, as her children attended services on the weekdays as well. For an aspiring professional musician, the demarcation between sacred and secular music was less emphatic. Life in the church offered no sustainable income, and the only other venues for a freelancer were taverns, gentlemen's clubs, dance halls, and brothels, most of which employed a pianist during all working hours to promote a cozy parlor atmosphere. Joplin's mother remained as a singular inspiration throughout his life and made her family's music available for weddings, funerals, and various celebrations. Scott's brother Robert is said to have harbored a keen interest in composition as well.

As a young man, Joplin was generally esteemed by his

[5] Addison W. Reed, Scott Joplin, Pioneer, The Black Perspective in Music, Vol. 3 No. 1 (Spring, 1975)

community as a "faithful, sincere person,"[6] and working on both sides of the available musical spectrum did not cause apparent antagonism from the church. Following a regimen of self-instruction at the piano, he attended the Orr School for a brief period and taught music to younger students.

By 1882, Florence had saved enough to purchase a piano for the house, a square grand, popular in 19th century homes. The instrument was later replaced by a similar model despite the square grand's value as furniture that generally exceeded its usefulness for musical quality.

In terms of instruction, Joplin was fortunate enough to catch the eye of instructor Julius Weiss around the age of 11, and Joplin was so proficient that Weiss offered to train him classically without charge. Little is known of Weiss' own background, except that he likely received conservatory training in Saxony before departing for America. Weiss could have been a German Jewish immigrant, but Christian Protestantism dominated German religious culture, suggesting possible Lutheran origins. Either way, he served as a family tutor for lumberman Colonel R.W. Rodgers, and he passed on much of his standard curriculum to Joplin. The generous teacher played the classics for Joplin and spoke glowingly of the European repertoire, including the most famous

---
[6] Addison W. Reed

operas of the day. Recent works of Richard Wagner and Giuseppe Verdi were taking Germany and Italy by storm, and the excellent foundation offered by Weiss served Joplin well in the latter's larger compositions of the same genre through the decades.

In his teen years and throughout the 1880s, Joplin put his associations with teachers and other aspiring artists to the test by arranging a tour of the Midwest and Northeast. As he gained more abilities on various instruments, he gathered likeminded musicians for various performing groups. Reputed to have been a quality vocalist as well, Joplin assumed the lead position with some of these ensembles, while for others, he manned the piano or played one of the cornet parts.

This early touring regimen served as the perfect laboratory for his developing composition skills as well. In his early career, his original pieces and arrangements were heard in locations where musical mistakes or harsh critics were unlikely to cause long-term harm to a novice building his craft. As a new ragtime pianist from Texarkana, the venues were not elegant performance halls, and the audiences of the rural South were far less formal than those of a European style concert. Indeed, the bulk of Joplin's performance experiences in the early years came almost solely from the town's rougher institutions.

The first tour's launch date is unknown. He may have remained in Texarkana up to 1888, where he purportedly served as a teacher at the Texarkana Negro School. At the time, he played first cornet in the Queen City Concert Band. His principal passion as a performer was tied up in the fortunes of his best ensemble to date, the Texas Medley Quartette, which he led from the piano unless a cornet was needed. The "Quartette" had been assembled four years prior, so the group was well-rehearsed by the year of their first tour, even as the personnel of the quartet would not remain set uniformly for four performers. Originally, the ensemble enlisted the assistance of two Joplin brothers, Will and Robert, but membership varied through the years, and it even reached a cast of eight at various times. Baritone Pleasant Jackson served as the vocal front man, and in the early years the group featured "Southern plantation and jubilee songs."[7]

Joplin employed a savvy approach to promotion when it came to the materials sent ahead beforehand. Upon their arrival at each new city, the ensemble appeared early in the morning at the offices of community newspapers, unannounced, and performed a brief excerpt for the staff. Church performances were held for a fee, but they performed for tips at local hotels and busked in the parks and along the streets. In time, they found official

[7] Russ Tarby, Scott Joplin's Forgotten Parlor Songs, The Syncopated Times – www.syncopatedtimes.com/scott-joplins-forgotten-parlor-songs/

representation in the St. Louis artist management agency of Oscar Dame, and it is believed that Joplin relocated to that city in 1885. Known as the "Gateway to the West," St. Louis afforded opportunities found in few other music centers, and Joplin was soon appearing as a pianist at the Silver Dollar Saloon.

In a fairly successful run for a first tour, Dame sent Joplin's ensemble through Cedar Rapids and Omaha, then on to Chicago, Cleveland, and Boston. Reviews were generally excellent, and one Cleveland paper praised the ensemble's "delightful harmonies."[8] Perhaps the most important performance of the tour from a promotional standpoint was an appearance on the outer boundary of the Chicago World's Fair, the Columbian Exhibition of 1893. Many attractions were held on the fair's periphery, including the Wild West Show of Buffalo Bill Cody, complete with a Native American contingent.

The venue offered to the Texas Medley Quartette undoubtedly carried racial implications as well, but despite being restricted to the fair's outskirts, Joplin left a strong impression on those who attended his ensemble's performances, and it was there that he established a close friendship with fellow rag pianist Otis Saunders. Joplin seldom wrote his compositions down, assuming that their usefulness would only extend to the performances at hand,

---

[8] Russ Tarby

but Saunders convinced him otherwise, and from that point on, new pieces were committed to paper.

Saunders and Joplin returned to St. Louis together after the successes Joplin enjoyed in Chicago. Additional advantages from the Chicago experience included live performances of famous artists he previously knew only by reputation. Chief among them was a band concert led by John Philip Sousa. The latest musical forms and popular songs were in full force through the run of the fair, and Joplin returned to St. Louis up to date with a grasp of new industry standards.

Sousa

Although the core repertoire remained a collection of folk tunes, cakewalks, and minstrel songs, Joplin was quick to arrange new tunes of the day and mix them into the performance. Among the hits of the late 19th century were songs by noted composer Joseph Tabrar, whose song *Daddy Wouldn't Buy Me a Bow Wow* became a rage on both sides of the Atlantic, with audiences joining in what are known today as "conga lines," echoing the barking of a dog every time the phrase "bow wow" rolled around on the verse. Added to the repertoire list were the first two Joplin songs ever to be published: *Please Say You Will* and *A Picture of Her Face*. When they were heard by two Syracuse publishers, M.L. Mantell Publishers put the former into print on February 20, 1895, and the Leiter Bros. released the latter in July of the same year.

Tabrar

Sedalia

"No doubt Joplin could play "ragged time," as it was first called because of its bouncing bass and syncopated right hand, as bumptiously as the next man. But by the time he began writing his rags down in the late 1890s, they had obviously become objects of care, even personal meaning for him." – William Bender, "Scott Joplin: From Rags to Opera," *Time* magazine (1975)

In the mid-1890s, Joplin relocated once more, this time to the smaller community of Sedalia, Missouri. Questioning the wisdom of such a move to a smaller location at the height of his career search may be an error, because Sedalia served St. Louis in the same way Branson did the city of Nashville in the 20th century. The town of 15,000 featured numerous music publishers and a surprising number of performance venues, including at least 20 restaurants, 31 saloons, and eight hotels. Joplin was fortunate to land employment in a tavern doubling as a gambling establishment, because the level of competition in Sedalia was high and featured a glut of good ragtime pianists, which led Joplin to recognize shortcomings in his own playing and musicianship that required upgrading. Where St. Louis was a showcase of talent for new music, Sedalia was considered the "cradle of ragtime"[9] in the early years. Among the ragtime pianists of the era, a contingent of the best could always be found there, including Saunders, Turpin, and Louis Chauvin.

[9] S. Brunson Campbell, R.J. Carew, Sedalia, Missouri; Cradle of Ragtime, Doctor Jazz – www.doctorjazz.co.uk/page34a.html

A portrait of Chauvin

It is believed that Joplin had arrived in Sedalia by 1894, but anecdotal information suggests that he had lived there before, finishing his secondary education at Lincoln High School in an earlier part of life. Since the school's records were destroyed by fire, no evidence of his attendance exists, but either way he was about 25 when he got to town at that time. He was almost entirely unknown, unpublished on any sizeable scale, and was at best an average pianist by national standards. His skill at the cornet was far worse. The reason he appeared in Sedalia at all can be answered in part by its geography. The community sat on a railroad line to Kansas City, a distance of only 40 miles. The employment opportunities were excellent, and the cost of living was lower than in the city. Many of the 15,000 residents were black, and the town's structures remained largely untouched from the Civil War. Joplin would end up remaining there until the early 20th century. Perhaps a sense of nostalgia helped draw him to Sedalia, and he may have assumed that the less worldly audience would be more forgiving of his piano skills than people in the metropolitan centers.

Furthermore, Joplin was not done with the idea of a formal education, even as he maintained his ambition to join the elite of the classical music world. The solution for elevating his mediocre performance levels could also be found in Sedalia, as the George R. Smith College for Negroes had been established nearly a decade earlier and included a Bachelor of Arts degree track in several disciplines, including music. The land was given by the founder's daughters to the Freedmen's Aid and Southern Education Society of the Methodist Church, and students hailed from Missouri, Kansas, and Oklahoma. Sedalia, with its musical leanings, became one of the first towns in the South to construct a black college.

Not only did Joplin's technical understanding and performance skills improve remarkably from his participation in the college's first class, but he took his hand at mentoring several students as well. He is said to have possessed "perfect pitch," the ability to phonate any requested pitch without exterior prompting or cues.

Among his other gifts was the ability to identify the underlying of the structure of music as he heard it, without the need of a keyboard. This grasp of advanced music theory connected to audial recognition would serve him well. At one point during the experience, he seemed optimistic in his bid to become a European-style concert pianist and composer. Piano studies were taken with Mrs. Minnie Jackson, while theory and composition instruction were overseen by a Professor Murray. During these formal studies, he remained unwilling to break away from the vocal and dance forms of his culture such as the cakewalk and the two-step. In Sedalia, as in numerous other communities, the cakewalk became exceedingly popular, and a general get-together based on the step provided a fitting end to a festive day. Joplin himself led such rousing events by instituting widely advertised "pretentious"[10] competitions for ragtime pianists at the Black 400 Ball. As a rule, he emerged as the eventual winner.

Joplin's first songs brought significant notoriety, negating any latent disappointment from living in a rural town. Well-established in Sedalia, a local newspaper once hailed him as "one of the best pianists in the world,"[11] although numerous later accounts did not grant him the same esteem in larger venues. Despite all the

[10] S. Brunson Campbell, R.J. Carew, Doctor Jazz
[11] Scott Joplin, last fm, Biography – www.last.fm/music/Scott+Joplin/+wiki

improvements garnered at the college, Joplin is said to have still lacked a total mastery over the craft of notation by the end of the decade. In his ragtime performances, he doubtlessly embellished the rhythm at the core of each piece, but printed examples from his notes show only the basic, unembroidered versions. The syncopated rhythms were a natural part of Joplin's playing, but he could not technically write them out on paper.

Following the tour that led to his first two publications in Syracuse, he returned home, and through the inspiration of Otis Saunders, he penned and published a piano piece entitled *The Great Crush Collision March.* The title was inspired by an infamous train collision in northeastern Texas. Within the following two years, he was able to sell six songs for piano to various publishers.

Joplin's first collection of piano rags, entitled *Original Rags*, was published near the end of the decade in Sedalia. It was here that he learned his first lesson in the cutthroat competition for song credit prevalent in all genres of published music. Through a scant association at best, Joplin was forced to share credit for the collection with an arranger named Charles N. Daniels despite having composed the pieces himself.

Unwilling to suffer a second such occurrence, he began to consult with a young Sedalia lawyer named Robert

Higdon to negotiate exclusive rights for future works. Joplin's primary publishing relationship was with John Stark & Son, a successful association that would last through the rest of the 19th century and beyond. In the summer of 1899, Stark first heard Joplin play what would become one of the two most famous works of his career, the *Maple Leaf Rag*. Though he was the sole composer, Joplin had nevertheless sought out the advice of Otis Saunders who believed his friend had created a career-altering work. Immediately taken with the piece, Stark invited him to play it again at his music store. A small group was present, and a young child danced as Joplin played it publicly for the first time. The *Maple Leaf Rag* attained almost immediate success and became the first work to provide Joplin with ongoing income.

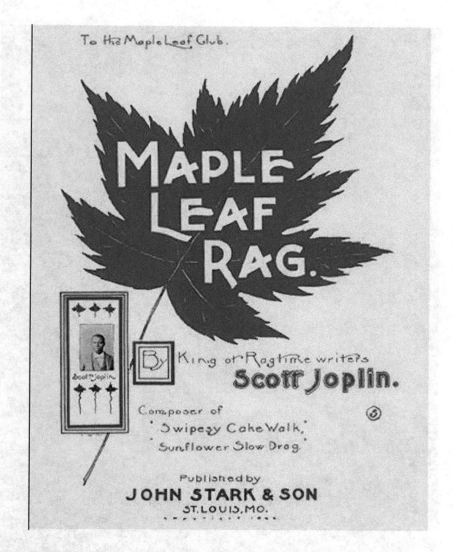

The third edition of *Maple Leaf Rag*

John Stark

In the same year, a second piece emerged that rivaled the first, known in the present day as *The Entertainer*. Stark, not generally willing to offer extensive royalties after the initial purchase, paid Joplin one cent per copy, and the composer earned $360 per year from sales of *The*

Entertainer for the remainder of his life. *The Maple Leaf Rag*, on the other hand, went on to become the highest selling piece of ragtime music in history, earning royalties from over one million copies.

Due in part to these pieces, the ragtime genre overtook the country and opened the door for Joplin's future works. These included the *Peacherine Rag*, *The Chrysanthemum*, the *Heliotrope Bouquet*, and *Euphonic Sounds*. The Maple Leaf, a gentlemen's club in Sedalia where Joplin often played, was delighted with the title and reveled in the local fame brought on by the success of their adopted son.

In 1899, Joplin married Belle Hayden, a widower, after which the two had a baby daughter who lived only a few weeks. Rumors persisted about Joplin having been in a previous marriage, but nobody in Joplin's inner circle ever validated its existence.

Throwing himself into a greater work regimen, he collaborated with student and fellow composer Arthur Marshall on a cakewalk project entitled *The Swipesy Cakewalk* in 1900. Marshall would continue to be an important association as composer Scott Hayden's roommate for years growing up through high school. Hayden was related by law to Belle Hayden, and he collaborated with Joplin on several successful rags. When Joplin arrived in Sedalia, he had stayed with the Marshall family during his search for housing.

Scott Hayden

Both Hayden and Marshall excelled under his tutelage, playing at the Maple Leaf and Nellie's Hall. Like Joplin, Marshall had trained as a classical pianist at Smith College, and as a classical player he took the opportunity to comment on Joplin's dexterity. In ragtime, the left hand handles both bass line and harmony, requiring rapid movement. Joplin's left hand, according to Marshall, "swung exceedingly well."[12]

In 1900, Stark published the Marshall and Joplin collaboration. It is suggested that Stark himself chose the title for this piece and used the photograph of an unidentified shoe shine boy on the front cover. According

---

[12] All Music, Arwulf, Arthur Marshall – www.allmusic.com/artist/arthur-marshal-mn-0000610335

to the publisher, the subject of the photo wore a "cookie swiping"[13] expression.

Taking note the migration of composers and pianists from Sedalia back to St. Louis, Stark also opened an office there in order to continue his collaborations with Joplin, Marshall, and others who eventually returned to the busier city. Naturally, Sedalia has never forgotten Joplin's presence in the town or his influence on the national interest in ragtime that emanated from their community. To this day, a high school in the town bears his name.

[13] All Music, Arwulf

Kevin Saff's picture of Joplin's house in St. Louis

Moving Forward

"A typical Joplin rag has a disciplined arrangement of repeats and returns not unlike that of the march, and a similar duple tune signature. Jazz probably got its start, Schuller believes, when saloon pianists who could not read music began improvising rags they had heard." – William Bender, "Scott Joplin: From Rags to Opera," *Time* magazine (1975)

Between 1900 and 1903, Joplin and Belle continued working through difficulties in their marriage, but the composer remained productive. In addition to his work with Stark, he gained the endorsement of Alfred Ernst, an important figure in St. Louis circles. The second conductor of the St. Louis Choral and Symphonic Society that later established the St. Louis Symphony Orchestra, the German-born pianist and conductor was an ideal association for raising Joplin's prestige as a serious artist. Publicly declaring him a genius, Ernst justified Joplin's output of ragtime pieces for piano, reminding listeners that it was only an innocent "pastime"[14] while he considered more serious projects. In America, the gold standard for opera, the top genre in all classical music, was Richard Wagner and his "music dramas," and Ernst

---

[14] Classical Net, Scott Joplin – www.classical.net/music/comp.lst/joplin.php

preached that Joplin, despite being black and trapped in a lower form of musical art, aspired to the greatness of the German master.

Largely unknown at the time was that Joplin did indeed aspire to become an opera composer in a musical style ultimately contrary to the styles of his upbringing. However, he intended to force a tradition of nearly 300 years to accept his alien music form into its canon. The miniature piano rags had bolstered his local popularity, and he did not stop writing them. Joplin maintained an optimistic view that the folk forms of black America would find their own place as respected classical genres, and that he could essentially convince Europe to come to him, rather than the other way around. However, white audiences remained staunch in their refusal to accept the "blend of European classical style and African American harmonies and rhythm."[15] At the worst, black music of the streets and taverns was contaminated by what elitists saw as a base culture, and at best it was considered to be of a "frivolous"[16] nature, lacking enlightenment.

From 1900-1903, Joplin published *The Entertainer*, *Elite Syncopations*, and *March Majestic*, among other works, and by 1901, he had composed *Sunflower Slow Drag* in collaboration with Scott Hayden. Insistent on altering the

[15] Library of Congress, Scott Joplin, 1868-1917 – www.loc.gov/item/ihas.200035815
[16] Library of Congress

public image of his black dance miniatures, Joplin continued to publish ragtime as classical music with an accented bass and "hard-driving melodies."[17] Stark was equally unapologetic, and he established a company called House of Classic Rags in 1901. Nonetheless, even the establishment of the International Ragtime Foundation was unable to turn the tide.

With a seemingly bottomless well of inspiration, Joplin's compositions continued to emerge on a regular schedule. Residing in St. Louis and being well-acquainted with all the best pianists in town, he realized that he would never possess superior piano skills in such a competitive environment. This reality likely pushed him further into an extended regimen of composition. He rarely performed in the city, but he established a well-regarded presence within the musical community. Considered by all who knew him as a refined individual, "quiet, serious, jolly, but not frivolous,"[18] his sense of humility led to numerous collaborations regardless of his partners' standing in the industry.

During his time in St. Louis, he rose to a level of prestige as the best composer of the ragtime genre along with James Scott and Joseph Lamb, a white composer writing in the black style. Joplin was reluctant to enter into

[17] All About Jazz, Scott Joplin Biography – www.musicians.allaboutjazz.com/scottjoplin

[18] Edward A. Berlin, Scott Joplin Sedalia: New Perspectives, *Black Music Research Journal*, Vol.; 19 No. 2, Papers of the 1989 National Conference on Black Music Research

unseemly squabbles over composer's credit, so he was a generous colleague to younger artists seeking a foothold. With his publishing associations, he assisted many of them in obtaining their first printed offerings for public consumption. Another account affirms Joplin's extreme adherence to social graces and his generally friendly demeanor, but at the same time it contradicted other descriptions by suggesting that he "never smiled in his life."[19] The same source went on to claim that the composer possessed a special gift that enabled him to avoid making enemies through his entire career. He purportedly shunned conflict of any sort, as a "kitten could knock him down."[20]

[19] Edward A. Berlin
[20] Edward A. Berlin

Lamb

As Joplin labored to fuse black and European art forms through the lofty genre of opera, he made the same effort with ballet and rural black dance. In 1902, he completed and published *Ragtime Dance* for a small dance ensemble of four couples and a singing narrator. Arthur Marshall assisted with the orchestration, and Joplin even included elements of his own choreography despite having a scant background in dance.

Stark was less amenable to experimental ventures into dance and opera than he was to the current rage of piano ragtime, and he sensed that the new work would fail from a financial standpoint, which was by necessity the publisher's guiding principle. However, Joplin had a fierce advocate in Stark's daughter, Eleanor Stark, who happened to be a professional-level pianist with stellar academic credentials and a history of European study with the legendary Moritz Moszkowski. More than an advocate for Joplin's music, she became an invaluable advisor for his work in preparation for introducing it to her business-minded father. It is believed that at one point, Eleanor convinced him to remain in business as a publisher, a decision that enabled him to put the wildly successful *Maple Leaf Rag* in print.

Moszkowski

Nevertheless, John Stark remained only half convinced,

publishing *Ragtime Dance* in a truncated form. His instinct for financial caution was in the end justified, as the experimental dance work failed to gather a wide audience.

Undeterred, Joplin continued his effort to expand black song and dance forms without sacrificing personal success. As a proponent of education for his race in the same kind of manner eloquently promoted by Booker T. Washington, he seized upon an important event in order to publish a piano rag entitled *The Strenuous Life.* Washington sought to elevate the conditions of black people through a systematic and national upgrade of practical education. Among whites, the fear of equality seemed to be approaching reality, so when President Theodore Roosevelt invited Washington to the White House, the sight of a black man entering a seat of government that those of his color were forced to build only a few years earlier was intolerable to many whites. As an artist, Joplin felt a deep cultural attachment to every work, and *The Strenuous Life* was based on a speech Roosevelt delivered three years prior. In it, the president touted the benefits of striving for a successful life and nation.

For Stark, any time spent on experiments or side ventures was time that could be spent composing another successful rag. *Ragtime* was a financial success at a time that black operas did not yet exist as a genre, so Joplin's attempts to unite black music to more "elite" forms of music frustrated the business side of things. Ultimately, however, the composer persisted with his first attempt at an extended opera, and due to Joplin's affinity for relevant cultural events, the meeting between Booker T. Washington and President Roosevelt seemed the ideal topic despite the political polarization that ensued. *A Guest of Honor* was completed by 1903, and a copyright application was sent to the Library of Congress, without the usually included score. This may indicate that Joplin erroneously believed it would be published before the submission. *A Guest of Honor* was the first widely publicized attempt at composing a quasi-European opera based on events involving African Americans. George Gershwin's *Porgy and Bess* would not come around for a few more decades.

The fate of *A Guest of Honor* ended up being a grim one despite its optimistic start. A tour of the Midwest was arranged for a series of performances, involving a cast of 30, making it an expensive venture for a lengthy tour. However, the opportunity was a blessing in that it was Joplin's first tangible opportunity to promote black operatic music before audiences riveted to the European tradition. In preparation, the work was rehearsed at the Crawford Theater of St. Louis, ahead of an itinerary that included numerous stops in Illinois, Missouri, Iowa, Kansas, and Nebraska. However, the production was closed by the middle of the tour. Either in Springfield, Illinois, or Pittsburg, Kansas, an unknown individual associated with the project made off with the box office receipts, leaving Joplin and *A Guest of Honor* in a state of bankruptcy.

OPERA HOUSE

Wednesday, Sept. 2

Scott Joplin's Rag Time Opera Co.
Management Welser & Amler

...... PRESENTING ......

A Guest of Honor

A Rag Time Opera in Two Acts by Scott
Joplin. Pretty Girls. Sweet Singers.
Elaborate Wardrobes. 16 People.

The only genuine Rag Time Opera ever
produced.

Prices, 25c, 35c, 50c, 75c

Seats at Chatterton's.

A 1903 advertisement for *A Guest of Honor*

It was Joplin who was held responsible for the losses.
The cast went unpaid, as did the boarding houses that

hosted them and the transportation upon which they depended for returning home. The remaining assets and all physical manifestations of the production were repossessed, including the music score itself. Had John Stark agreed to publish the opera based on the history of success with Joplin, the existing score would have been duplicated, easily replaced, and catalogued. It is believed that the national copyright office lost the only extant score, Stark possessed no surviving copy, and the composer's score was confiscated. Music historians have held out hope for a score to emerge from a yet unknown source, but the opera is now considered lost forever. Stark's refusal to preserve *A Guest of Honor* in print caused a severe break in his relationship with Joplin, one which was never fully repaired.

Meanwhile, Joplin's collaborations with Arthur Marshall continued, with Marshall serving as the pianist for the Scott Joplin Drama Company in St. Louis. He provided an orchestration for the *Ragtime Dance* as well, despite the work's inability to gather a national audience after repeated attempts. The two also collaborated on a piece generally regarded as one of Joplin's most beautiful, entitled *Lily Queen*.

Nevertheless, the loss of his opera devastated the otherwise successful composer. His broken state of mind was further exacerbated by the end of his marriage to

Belle Hayden. Joplin's income now depended on numerous short-term jobs in various venues, but he could not muster the funds with which to recoup *A Guest of Honor*.

With every facet of his life seemingly imploding at the same time, Joplin made one short visit to Chicago before a trip to Arkansas to visit relatives. There, he met the woman some have characterized as the love of his life, Freddie Bethena Alexander, who was 20 at the time. The two first met at the home of Freddie's parents, and their honeymoon consisted of a brief stay in several small towns where Joplin had arranged to play piano recitals. Having married almost immediately, such an itinerary could not be changed on short notice. The couple settled in Sedalia seven weeks later, only for the newly married Freddie to be confined to her bed at all times. What was in the beginning a simple cold resulted in complications of pneumonia. Joplin and his new wife were married for a total of 10 weeks before her death. The *Sedalia Weekly Conservator* of 1904 suggests that he remained at home and "administered to [her] every want,"[21] assisted by Freddie's sister, Lovie Alexander. Freddie's death was not unexpected, but the already fragile Joplin was further devastated. Following the internment at the "colored cemetery" of Morgan Street Baptist Church, he left

[21] Sedalia Weekly Conservator, Sedalia, MO, Sept. 16, 1904 – www.findagrave.com/memorial/82753051/freddie-joplin

Sedalia, never to return. It is possible that Freddie's remains have been moved to an unmarked grave elsewhere in the town. The reason for such a relocation is unclear.

In time, Joplin found enough work to recover financially from recent disasters, and he was invited to perform at the St. Louis World's Fair in 1904. That same year, he established a music company in the city with his new bride-to-be, Lottie Stokes. His first published piece after the loss of Freddie Alexander was entitled *Bethena*, Freddie's middle name. A complicated piece featuring brooding harmonies in comparison to his brighter works, the tribute to his late wife is set in a minor key producing a dark, slow waltz.

A cover for *Bethena* believed to have used a wedding picture of Freddie

After months of emotional "faltering,"[22] Joplin returned to his winning ways by composing several bestselling piano rags. 1906 was largely taken up by an extended visit to Europe, during which Joplin composed virtually

---

[22] Scott Joplin, last fm

nothing. Whether the logistics of the journey made composing difficult, or whether he was empty of inspiration after losing his wife and a young child, is unclear, but the value of the time spent in Europe was immense as Joplin encountered the most authentic examples of the forms he admired. He seemingly returned to America somewhat rejuvenated.

During a brief period in 1907 spent in Chicago with Sedalia friend Arthur Marshall, he co-wrote *Heliotrope Bouquet* with Louis Chauvin. It would be the only published work for which the brilliant pianist Chauvin was ever granted credit before he died several months later.

That same year, Joplin moved to New York City. With all the variations and hideous contortions being practiced on the pure form of ragtime by ignorant pianists, Joplin concluded that he should write a textbook clarifying correct performance practices and outlining the musical grammar of the piano rag genre. Such a decision was appropriate, as he was once again at the top of the ragtime world. The document he produced, *The School of Ragtime,* served as both an instruction book featuring rhythms and examples of syncopation, harmonies common to the form, and suggested points of interpretations for live performances. Many ragtime aficionados took the text to heart, and Joplin's style was widely imitated.

The date of Joplin's marriage to business partner Lottie Stokes is unclear. A few sources believe the marriage occurred in 1909, but the widower census did not include the marriage as it should have. Joplin resided in a boarding house at 128 W. 129th Street in that year, and the couple was not placed together historically until a rental at 252 West 47th Street. However, that structure was a studio rather than a residence. The marriage may have taken place as much as four years after, and the two were barred from appearing in certain social circumstances without the certainty of marriage.

As Joplin began to play again, the problem of his performance levels once more became a topic of conversation. A 1911 issue of *New York Magazine* described his playing in glowing terms, and a well-known fellow pianist suggested that although Joplin only played his own works to the exclusion of all else, he certainly played them well. However, he added that Joplin played like "a stationary Indian,"[23] suggesting a static sense of movement. For the playing of ragtime, such a comment was not necessarily critical since the form requires a stable sense of tempo and the same rhythmic rigidity one might expect of a march.

---

[23] Scott Joplin, last fm

That said, fellow pianist Sam Patterson tersely insisted that his colleague had "never played well."[24] Artie Matthews, a song and ragtime composer, inferred that many St. Louis pianists took delight in performing Joplin's music at a higher level than that of the composer. Such comments may address Joplin's inability to break through his more provincial level of dexterity and command of touch. Another source theorized that he may have begun to feel the first effects of what ended up being syphilis.

As for the rigidity of the music, Joplin understood that his works were being taken up as a ragtime dance craze among whites, and if his music was serving as a dance accompaniment for well-clad amateurs, stability and restraint of tempo was paramount. Ragtime moved out of the black taverns and clubs, and onto the ballroom floors of wealthy, formal organizations. While Joplin had been unsuccessful in melding ragtime and its cultural roots to art forms popular among whites, dance sensations Irene and Vernon Castle accomplished it nearly overnight in the 1910s. Ragtime was either choreographed to its pure musical form or alloyed to other popular steps. These included the *Tango*, the *Grizzly Bear*, *Castle Walk*, and the *Maxixe*, often referred to as the *Mattchiche*. The ragtime waltz produced a series of variations under the

---

[24] Scott Joplin, last fm

category of "hesitation" waltzes, typified by Joplin's charming *Cinderella*.

THE TANGO OF TO-DAY

Irene and Vernon Castle

Little evidence suggests that Joplin increased his regimen of live performances because he missed the concert life. It is likely that he needed funds for his abiding interest in African American opera. The bulk of his reasoning for a relocation to New York four years prior was to put the finishing touches on his new opera *Treemonisha*, and to work on mounting a subsequent performance. The opera was the all-consuming work of his later career, and the most important consideration of his professional life.

The opera's setting is a forest near an old slave plantation, and the character of Treemonisha is an 18-year old who has been taught to read by a white woman. Through her curiosity and newfound education, she leads her community against a horde of "conjurers who prey on ignorance and superstition."[25] Many who may or may not appreciate ragtime music in short piano pieces have avoided an encounter with *Treemonisha*, expecting a full length work based on the tavern-style syncopation, likely to become tedious after two hours. However, even though the score makes use of cultural dance forms, it is not a ragtime opera. To the contrary, many sections are quasi-European and generally considered to be a lovely example of a new American vocal paradigm. The structure is in keeping with European formats, and Joplin himself wrote the entire body of text, the libretto. Few composers have chosen to undertake such a feat outside of Wagner, and Joplin went one better by choreographing much of the dance aspects as well.

[25] Larry Melton, Scott Joplin's Treemonisha: The First Stagings Remembered, March 29, 2019, Syncopated Times – www.syncopatedtimes.com/scott-joplins-treemonisha-the-first-stagings-remembered

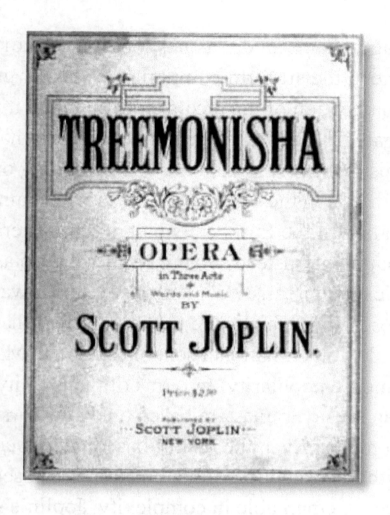

The cover of the score

Undertaking a project of such scope was indeed virgin territory, A *Guest of Honor* aside. Joplin was not innately an operatic person, despite having heard major works through Weiss and having attended watered down touring versions, most without orchestra. He certainly admired the form, sought a place in it for his own reputation, and considered it a way of "the raising of the race through education."[26] However, whether he loved it on the same

[26] Klaus Dieter-Gross, The Politics of Scott Joplin's "Treemonisha" – *Amerikastudien/American Studies*, Vol. 45 No. 3 (2000) Universitätsverlag (WINTER)

level as rag remains an open question. In terms of racial advancement, the art form's importance was far greater in terms of perception of the race's elevation than it was in tangible gains. Historically, he may or may not have realized his own work's share in "the beginning of black modernism."[27] On the other hand, those who claimed an understanding of the European opera world generally missed that point, instead seizing on the libretto as "simplistic and unrealistic."[28] This assessment was grossly and purposefully unfair as the concept of the folk tale figures widely in all national schools of opera. Many enjoy immense popularity. In terms of plausibility, the Wagnerian music dramas are based on a potpourri of European myths. Even the reality-based *opera seria* of Verdi, with the exception of his Shakespearian settings, were often unremarkable in complexity. Joplin's simple folk tale that carried a hefty social message for all disenfranchised cultures appears to owe Europe no apology whatsoever.

Despite the opera's setting in the post-war Reconstruction era, Joplin's text makes scarcely any mention of the Civil War. One brief reference mentions an "unnamed war,"[29] then moves on. The forward-looking score, obsessed with racial education, excludes the white

---

[27] Klaus-Dieter Gross
[28] Klaus-Dieter Gross
[29] Klaus Dieter Gross

world entirely, conceptually and literally on stage. In the absence of overt strife between the races, the most obvious choice for a general topic, *Treemonisha* is still an "outspokenly political work."[30] As it was for Booker T. Washington, the politics remain largely internal and deal with a race elevating itself from within, requesting and receiving no assistance. As characters of early operas wore symbolic garb and headwear to mark them metaphorically, such as "mercy" or "hope," the heroic character of *Treemonisha* might as well do the same with the crown of "education." Through such opportunity, she frees her people without sacrificing their character, dignity, or identity. Joplin himself kept his personal policies close to the vest, but his wish to be accepted as a "cultural as well as cultured"[31] leader himself is well documented. Whatever his specific politics, his desire for blacks to "acquire practical intelligence"[32] is overt through his two operatic attempts.

In his move to the wealthier city, Joplin's rift with John Stark grew wider as the publisher balked at the idea of a second opera after refusing to publish the first. A possibility existed that his former promoter might publish an excerpt with no royalties distributed, but nothing more. In his search for support, Joplin acted too loosely with the

---

[30] Klaus Dieter-Gross

[31] Klaus Dieter-Gross

[32] Klaus Dieter Gross

work, sending a score to several possible promoters. One was the editor of *American Musician*, an important music magazine of the era. The response was encouraging, as the resulting article declared *Treemonisha* to be "the most American opera ever composed."[33]

While he waited for new publishers to peruse the work and respond to his request for publication, Joplin continued on other projects. He composed the music for a vaudeville act, a work of musical theater, a symphonic work, and a piano concerto. To his disappointment, none of these works were ever published, and all the manuscripts are presumed lost. This unfortunate and ongoing habit of letting scores slip away should have been cured by the fate of *A Guest of Honor*. However, as before, a price was paid for Joplin's response to Stark's hesitation. In passing around so many scores of the second opera, he was not able to keep track of them or guard them from being plagiarized. One was sent to the legendary Irving Berlin, who, according to Joplin, stole an important section of the *Treemonisha* finale. Berlin held on to the score for some time before returning it, at last explaining that he could not find a good use for it. However, he copyrighted *Alexander's Ragtime Band* two months before Joplin copyrighted the opera on May 9, 1911. Berlin's new hit was noticeably similar to the

[33] Scott Joplin.org, Scott Joplin – the Man and His Music – www.scottjoplin.org/joplin-biography.html

rousing end of Joplin's work, entitled *Marching Onward*. Various modern scholars have debated the hypothetical results of a court case had it been conducted in the present day. However, despite his prestige as a ragtime composer, Joplin was in no position to challenge Berlin, a white legend with an enormous reserve of financial, legal, and public support. The two likely knew one another, but it was a gossip columnist who first publicized Joplin's displeasure. Berlin answered with an emphatic denial, and little more was heard of it.

Berlin

In the world of piano ragtime and dance, Joplin may have succeeded in his mission to join with white society's art forms through Irene and Vernon Castle's dance careers. However, he enjoyed no such opportunity in the opera world, which remained a white and "staid classical venue."[34] As it is in the present, opera in the early 20th century was founded on strict theatrical and musical traditions based in whatever era first produced the work. In Italian opera, foreign elements were occasionally sprinkled in when the contrast of a foreign character was necessary. America itself was considered a secondary opera market, and it lacked even a national opera house until the first years of the Metropolitan in New York. The Americas could not at that time hope to impose any new traditions on the predominantly Italian, German, and French genre. Even in the "New World," ragtime, with which the opera was misconstrued, could not escape the brand of "cheap, vulgar, and facile black music."[35] No publisher would accept the 230-page *Treemonisha* piano and vocal score, and no orchestration was yet completed. Despite submitting the title to the Library of Congress for a fee of $1, he soon offered it for sale at $2.50. Even at such an absurdly low price, no one came forward.

---

[34] All About Jazz, Scott Joplin
[35] All About Jazz, Scott Joplin

A performance of *Treemonisha* with piano accompaniment, 11 principal singers, and a chorus of 40 fell through, and the best Joplin could manage was a read through with the public invited to attend. This skeletal "performance" of the opera was essentially no more than a rehearsal, and it lacked the stage action. For an operatic work containing dance forms, such an event was deflating and uninformative for any likely promoter. Even the logistics of the read through were a failure. Meant to be held on July 4, 1913, the press advertised the *Treemonisha* workshop as taking place in Bayou, New Jersey, a nonexistent community and an obvious misspelling of Bayonne.

Indeed, given the lack of advertising sent out by the composer himself, one might suspect that Joplin was so unhappy with the production's condition that he hoped no one would attend. He was never to hear his dearest work in its entirety or with full orchestra even though he finally completed an orchestration. Lester Walton, in a later eulogy, suggests that Joplin had in the previous year met with black opera composer Harry Lawrence Freeman, a noted authority on the international genre who produced musical theater works as well. A conductor, impresario, and teacher, Freeman was the ideal choice for assisting this one-of-a-kind work so far out of the mainstream. The founder of multiple music schools and small opera companies, Freeman was the first to successfully produce an African American opera, *Epthalia.* He came to be known as the "Black Wagner,"[36] the highest praise imaginable for an American opera composer, let alone one who was African American.

Freeman

One might suppose that having experienced greater success than his colleague over the course of a much longer life, Freeman might occupy the position in history that Joplin so fervently sought to hold. However, Freeman's most famous works, such as *Nada the Lily*,

Allah, and *The Zulu King* tend to favor distant and conceptual black topics. His American works often center on the personal and romantic aspects of the village tale and do not so obsessively speak to those larger and literal social matters taken up by Joplin.

Freeman advised Joplin to make extensive rewrites of the opera, which the composer set out to do at once. What remains in the present day is a vocal and piano score from that year, but Joplin's own orchestration became lost due to another instance of self-neglect. Modern musicologists are uncertain as to whether the existing score contains Joplin's latest alterations based on Freeman's advice. No public mention was made of *Treemonisha* for the following two years. The entire compositional and promotional process had lasted over a decade, and it was undertaken at the composer's personal expense. With the opera's failure, Joplin was again heartbroken and poor, having suffered a nervous breakdown.

Joplin's Final Years

"When I'm dead twenty-five years, people are going to begin to recognize me." – Scott Joplin

Joplin and his third wife, Lottie, continued to operate their publishing company through 1913. The details of his marriage to Stokes were largely unrecorded, even in the New York Archives of that year, but it is known that

Lottie remained with him for the rest of his life.

In 1914, Joplin composed his final ragtime piano piece, the *Magnetic Rag*. Still harboring bitter disappointment over the fate of *Treemonisha*, he took one opportunity to hear a symphonic excerpt from the opera's various dances performed at the nearby Martin-Smith Music School on West 136th Street. Ironically, the performance was held just a few blocks away from his apartment. The ballet segment, entitled *Frolic of the Bears,* was a general disappointment.

No other projects of any scope occupied the deflated Joplin's attention. In 1916, he was physically weak and suffering mental deterioration, leading to his institutionalization. He was suffering from the long-term effects of syphilis, which he had unwittingly contracted decades earlier. Among the prevailing symptoms was "discoordination of the fingers,"[37] so his ability to play at all vanished over a brief period. Joplin's final scribbles of musical lines as the basis of intended works were accomplished in brief "bursts of lucidity"[38] at the Manhattan State Hospital. Various friends aided him in jotting the ideas down before sudden relapses ended the process.

After January 1917, Joplin never wrote another note, and

[37] Scott Joplin, last fm
[38] Scott Joplin, last fm

unfortunately, he never personally produced a true audio recording, so the nature of his playing is impossible to ascertain today. However, he did produce seven piano rolls, extended lengths of paper on which each note played corresponds to a perforation through the surface. The paper roll passes over a reading mechanism in a player piano known as the task bar, and each perforation triggers its assigned note as laid down by the performer. Piano rolls cannot reproduce the artistic finesse of individual performers, such as tone color, balance between melody and accompaniment, or the shaping of the phrase. However, the result is the best a listener can hear as a facsimile. In some cases, Joplin made early and late career piano rolls of pieces such as the *Maple Leaf Rag*. In the later examples, his abilities at embellishment seem to be enhanced from his youth, but the general state of his coordination had eroded. The last roll of *Maple Leaf Rag* clearly shows the progression of what was later known to be a spiral into dementia, paranoia, and physical paralysis.

Scott Joplin died on April 1, 1917, likely at the age of 49 or 50. The death certificate listed the cause of death as "dementia-paralytica-cerebral,"[39] but offered no further detail. Despite the esteem earned within his industry, Joplin's death did not make national headlines. By 1917,

---

[39] Encyclopedia.com, Scott Joplin, Composer, Pianist – www.encyclop0edia.com/people/literature-and-arts/music-popular-and-jazz-biographies/scott-joplin

ragtime was evolving into forms of modern jazz, and his credentials in the older style had begun to grow outdated. Furthermore, within days of his death, the U.S. was poised to enter World War I. All but forgotten, Joplin was buried at St. Michael's Cemetery in the Astoria section of Queens County, East Elmhurst, in New York. A memorial bench was later installed a few feet from his grave.

Many details about Joplin's personal life, which was always private in nature, will never be known. His lack of care when it came to tending to his own scores has made it impossible to fully assess his musical legacy, a legacy he likely assumed would never last. The obstacles to authentic research were worsened by the public abandonment of ragtime music, and a continuation of labeling black musical works as anomalous and inferior to classical norms.

A resurgence of interest in Joplin as an artist and ragtime as a genre came in the 1940s, during World War II. The nation was transfixed by the big band era, and jazz ensembles began to include older ragtime examples alongside more modern repertoires. A second wave of interest in the by then historical genre of ragtime came about in the 1970s, but even still, the lost opera *Treemonisha* never received its due until much further along.

Joplin's musical papers and unpublished manuscripts were willed to a friend serving as the executor of his estate. Wilbur Sweatman, a fellow musician and composer, took good care to keep them reasonably catalogued and safe from the elements, but he was perhaps overly generous in sharing them during a period in which ragtime had become passé. As a clarinetist, Sweatman was an eager aficionado of both ragtime and Dixieland, and he was the first black musician to record while employing the new name of "jazz." He died in 1961, and the ensuing legal battle between his sister and daughter caused the Joplin's original scores to "disappear under mysterious circumstances,"[40] never to be seen again.

The signature work of Joplin's life, *Treemonisha,* remained lost, generally misunderstood, disrespected, and shunned by Western classical organizations. Biographers, mistakenly characterizing the later years as an era of failure, erroneously turned to his Sedalia years as the richest source of study. This was due in part to the popular book written by Rudi Blesh and Harriet Janis, *They All Played Ragtime.* This account of Joplin's life covered the Sedalia and St. Louis years exclusively, treating the New York output as "anticlimactic."[41] The New York years

[40] Frank Powers, Wilbur Sweatman, Artist Biography, All Music – www.allmusic.com/artist/wilbur-sweatman-mn0000820923/biography
[41] Edward A. Berlin

lacked the details of his time in Sedalia and St. Louis, and they were negatively portrayed as being affected by disease, professional failure, and general depression in a city that came to forget him. By contrast, Joplin's time in Missouri was portrayed as flush with success, and that success was attested to by family, friends, and colleagues.

Blesh admitted to being uneasy about works that were composed in New York, including the *Wall Street Rag*. Ascribing the piece as Joplin's surrender to a heartless capitalist view, Blesh missed the simpler point altogether. Joplin obtained a job playing the piano for a club near the Financial District and made a note of it in the title. *Wall Street Rag* carried no more social significance other than a logistical one.

The dormant *Treemonisha* aside, Joplin composed over a dozen piano works in his final years, and he was far from forgotten by the leading black musicians of the city. Never intending for his New York tenure to be anything but a fundraising expedition for his opera, he nevertheless interacted with important figures such as William Spiller. The director of a successful vaudeville group called Six Musical Spillers, Spiller was college educated and played virtually every instrument in the modern orchestra. His wife was Isabel Taliaferro Spiller, who was prominent at the New England Conservatory of Music and Columbia University. Joplin presented these new contacts with a score of *Treemonisha*, and he appeared at the various black events held throughout the city. Through Spiller, he met editors of newspapers and emerging arts magazines. The *American Musical Journal* subsequently attempted to duplicate Alfred Ernst's promotion of Joplin as a serious classical musician. According to a feature article, "He doesn't like the light music of the day; he is delighted with Beethoven and Bach…his compositions, though syncopated, smack of the higher cult."[42] Such was a typical print media account, making excuses for Joplin's love of syncopation. The error was based on the overtness of Joplin's ragtime syncopation, and a lack of recognition that Beethoven and Bach were masters of the same device, merely couched in a larger intellectual framework. Joplin played excerpts of *Treemonisha* for a popular vaudevillian named Bradford, who declared without reservation that the work was as "great as anything written by Mr. Wagner or Gounod."[43] The still unpublished and unperformed opera was referenced by Leslie Walton, an entertainment editor for the *New York Age*, who made mention of *Treemonisha* in his written eulogy upon Joplin's death.

As this indicates, all the ingredients necessary for national success in the ragtime genre's central venues were perfectly prepared. Joplin's career and reputation

[42] Edward A. Berlin
[43] Edward A. Berlin

were undone by his unceasing obsession with an opera no one in his era asked for or wanted to see.

In the wake of the Civil Rights Movement, writers in the 1970s began to look back at Joplin's career. Whereas Joplin and other artists in his time strove to meld black musical forms to the classical world, the revolutionary spirit of the 1960s and 1970s insisted upon it. In contrast to the earlier era's view of ragtime, the post-Reconstruction composers were no longer held to a lofty European model. In that way, the finer qualities of early black jazz and classical works at last shone through, and musicians like Joplin were validated apart from being compared to Bach, Mozart, and Beethoven.

Much of the initial interest emerged from the collegiate music world, where research most easily and inexpensively transitioned into live performance. For the works of Joplin, the most startling difference in the modern day was a parallel tribute and sign of welcome for *Treemonisha* beside iconic renditions of his piano rags in 1970. The tribute began when Joshua Rifkin, pianist, musicologist, and professor at Boston University, included Joplin rags on his piano recording for the greatly respected Nonesuch label. The effort was nominated for a Grammy award soon after.

Shortly after that, Joplin was inducted into the

Songwriters Hall of Fame by the National Academy of Popular Music, and ragtime pieces that had been forgotten for decades were collected and published in scholarly journals in 1971. One inclusion was a long-sought piano roll thought to have disappeared. It featured Joplin's *Silver Swan Rag*, thought to have been written in or around 1914. The sheet music was never published in his lifetime and was likely lost in the Sweatman litigation.

At long last, *Treemonisha* was given its first chance to be heard live in its entirety, half a century after its conception. The premiere was hosted in Atlanta, Georgia under the auspices of Morehouse College. The orchestration was provided by T.J. Anderson, who fashioned it from the piano and vocal score, and the performance was conducted by legendary choral conductor Robert Shaw. Among the luminaries present at the premier performance was the great pianist Eubie Blake, who had lived in Joplin's era. To accompany the premier performance, Morehouse formed an academic panel of "ragtime authorities"[44] to analyze *Treemonisha*. The group included classical songwriter William Bolcom, who provided a second orchestration to the opera. Although non-classical aficionados eagerly refer to the quip that talking about music is as useless as dancing to architecture, a legion of questions required answers in

[44] Larry Melton, Scott Joplin's Treemonisha: The First Stagings Remembered, March 29, 2019, Syncopated Times – www.syncopatedtimes.com/scott-joplins-Treemonisha-the-first-stagins-remembered

order to offer an authentic performance and fill in biographical gaps. Interest in the newly revived *Treemonisha* bloomed as a live performance was given at the Wolf Trap Theater of Washington, D.C. in August of 1972. A live performance followed in the same year at Southern Illinois University.

Ragtime itself received a boost from the 1973 George Roy Hill film *The Sting*, starring Robert Redford. In the general score, Joplin's piano rag, *The Entertainer*, figured prominently, becoming instantly familiar to people who weren't even fans of musicals in the first place. An adaptation of Joplin's famous rag was then created by composer and conductor Marvin Hamlisch, one of a select few to win a Grammy, an Emmy, Tony, and Oscar Award. Hamlisch went on to compose *A Chorus Line,* for which he won a Pulitzer Prize.

The Entertainer, the *Maple Leaf Rag* and other Joplin pieces are played in the modern day by students and professionals alike. *The Entertainer* was embraced by later generations as a fresh new work, and it reached the Billboard Hot 100 in 1974. Few seemed the slightest bit concerned that the music was not an authentic historical match for the setting of *The Sting*, belonging to an earlier era.

Kenneth MacMillan produced a ballet production for the

Royal Ballet in London on the works of Joplin. Entitled *Elite Syncopations*, the production was premiered at Covent Garden in October of 1974. Critics hailed the work as "MacMillan at his most playful."[45] *Elite Syncopations* had a negligible plot at best, but it served as a dance competition watched by other dancers, who are in turn watched by the live audience, an older version of the *Chorus Line* format. Through the evening, it featured a series of rags, cakewalks, and slow drags, all executed with "virtuosity and comic flair."[46] John Clifford of the Los Angeles Ballet choreographed a production entitled *Red Black Book* set to Joplin rags in a fully orchestrated performance.

Treemonisha appeared again in 1974 as part of the Scott Joplin Ragtime Festival, held annually since the 1970s in Sedalia, Missouri. Each spring, Joplin lovers and performers descend on the Missouri town from points across the globe. The crossover appeal of the work as part classical opera and part 19th century popular dance enabled it to avoid simple categorization. The jaunty Joplin style caught the attention of French audiences, who have for centuries demanded extensive choreography in their operatic repertoire.

In the same year the Wolf Trap production was held, the

---

[45] Kennethmacmillan.com, Elite Syncopations, 1974 – www.kennethmacmillan.com/elite-syncopations
[46] Kennethmacmillian.com

opera appeared on Broadway at the Uris Theater, where it ran for a successful two months. That said, the pinnacle for the play came from a Houston Opera production in 1975, featuring the masterful and elegant soprano Carmen Balthrop and a fine supporting cast. In her career, Balthrop performed the role of Treemonisha on multiple occasions in addition to her mainstream operatic roles. Composer Gunther Schuller conducted in Houston and created yet another orchestration employed in the performances. The Houston performance was broadcast, bringing *Treemonisha* to the attention of many listeners who had either not heard of it or musicians who had overlooked it. Eventually, the entire work was recorded by Deutsche Grammophon, a prestigious European label. In large part owing to such a strong and thorough production, Joplin was posthumously awarded a Pulitzer Prize for *Treemonisha* in 1976, an honor which would undoubtedly have stupefied the composer considering the ubiquitous rejection of the score in his lifetime.

Two films were produced on the life of Joplin near the end of the 1970s. In 1977, a biographical film simply entitled *Scott Joplin* was released by Motown Productions, starring Billy Dee Williams. The film went on to win a Pulitzer Prize. The second, *The Life of Scott Joplin*, premiered in Washington, D.C., and was short-lived. Some critics found the film overly romanticized, while others hailed it for its authenticity.

H. Wiley Hitchcock, a noted American musicologist, declared that Joplin's work stands as "the first American art music,"[47] emerging from the nation's people with no foreign influence. At the peak of Joplin mania, numerous schools and streets were renamed in his honor through various regions of the country. He has been widely forgotten since, but at the least the historical error of excluding him from the archives of the genre has been corrected. In 1983, Joplin received a postage stamp in the Black Heritage Commemorative Series, and four years later he was inducted into the Big Band and Jazz Hall of Fame.

Few fully produced productions of *Treemonisha* have appeared since the Houston effort of the mid-1970s, but the St. Louis Opera, known for its innovative programming, performed it in 2000. The work was of particular interest in that city due to Joplin's time spent there during one of his most creative periods. Two years later, his piano rolls were included by the National Recording Preservation Board in the Library of Congress Recording Registry.

Joplin's legacy rests upon a substantial collection of classic rags numbering in the hundreds, of which the most

[47] Addison Reed

popular are still *The Entertainer* and the *Maple Leaf Rag*. Rounding out the Joplin catalogue are a few songs with piano accompaniment, a set of Etudes or studies, and one extant operatic masterpiece. Given the existence of a well-informed performance of *Treemonisha*, the operatic style of Joplin has been well served in the present day. However, as often happens, vain or untrained pianists will use older genres to impress with their speed and general virtuosity at the expense of deeper expressions. According to Rudi Blesh, this form of "quack-virtuoso musical mayhem"[48] was already abundant among the pianists of Joplin's era. The uninitiated listener will, more often than not, recognize and admire speed and unmusical flair before profundity of phrase shaping, so the pianist with minimal artistic integrity is always tempted to pander to that. The only model for authentic performances is Joplin's instructional document on ragtime, setting the tempos at danceable levels. Outside of these, even his piano rolls are somewhat based on the calibration of the playback mechanism.

In a search for photographs of Joplin, only three have survived, and as for his views on art and the world, only a few firsthand quotations from the artist were preserved. The lack of pictures and quotes add to the sense that when he died, he believed he had been a failure. His austere

[48] Scott Joplin, last fm

photographs seem to affirm descriptions of him as "quiet, serious, and modest,"[49] forever ill at ease with small talk and rarely willing to divulge any information beyond the general topic in personal matters.

Some mistakenly claim that the genre of ragtime was invented by white musicians and merely copied by African Americans. If that theory was correct, they would have been obligated to create and choreograph the dance forms from which the music emerged as well. These neatly choreographed steps are unmistakably African American and were unlikely to have been danced without music while waiting for a white composer to furnish it. The instrument most present behind the dance culture was the banjo, and it was this flavor that Joplin transferred to the piano so successfully. Dave Lewis, an author for All Music on the subject of Joplin, noted that the "intelligent, well-mannered, and well-spoken"[50] artist "elevated banjo piano-playing"[51] from low entertainment associated with saloons and brothels into a beloved and enduring American music form. The term "rag" was once a disparaging adjective used by white purists to describe black music, but Joplin raised its prestige and emblemized the genre, as John Phillip Sousa did the march.

No work of Joplin was created outside of his "culturally

[49] Scott Joplin.org

[50] Scott Joplin.org

[51] All Music.com

attached"[52] creative nature. His hopes that such music would speak to the issues and needs of the 19th century were most emphatic in his struggle for a nationalist art form that would serve black people in the wake of Reconstruction. The mixture of white and black musical elements was initially rejected, which should come as no surprise, but eventually that mixture was embraced. Of course, that popularity would only come more than half a century after the equality movements led by Booker T. Washington, W.E.B. Du Bois, and Marcus Garvey.

Today, ragtime is hardly a popular genre, but even if the musical styles of the early 20th century are no longer necessary or appropriate for the mission of achieving civil rights, the music survives nonetheless. *Treemonisha* still stands ably on its own as a historical reminder, and even if the opera and hundreds of piano rags no longer wield the social impact on behalf of modern racial equality that they once did, their place in the repertoire is secure. As new musical forms are joined to cultural movements, Joplin's works can just as easily be appreciated for their beauty, in the same way his white counterparts have always been judged. In the end, an African American composer and child of a former slave successfully brought his repressed cultural genre to white audiences at a time when Jim Crow was prevalent throughout the South and racism

---

[52] Klaus Dieter-Gross

made it all but impossible for black artists to break through.

Online Resources

Other books about music by Charles River Editors

Other books about Scott Joplin on Amazon

Further Reading

All About Jazz, Scott Joplin Biography – www.musicians.allaboutjazz.com/scottjoplin

All Music, Scott Joplin, Artist Biography by Uncle Dave Lewis – www.allmusic.com/artist/scott-joplin-mn0000843212/biography

All Music, Arthur Marshall, Arwulf, - www.allmusic.com/artist/arthur-marshalkl-mn-00006103356

AZQuotes, Scott Joplin – www.azquotes.com/author/42237_Scott_Joplin

Berlin, Edward A., Scott Joplin's Treemonisha Years, *American Music*, Vol. 19 No. 3, Special Issue, University of Illinois Press

Berlin, Edward A., Scott Joplin in Sedalia: New Perspectives, *Black Music Research Journal*, Vol. 19 No. 2, Papers of the 1989 National Conference on Black

Music Research

Biography, Scott Joplin, Songwriter, Pianist (c. 1868-1917) – www.biography.com/musician/scott-joplin

Campbell, S., Brunson, Carew, R.J., Sedalia, Missouri; Cradle of Ragtime, Doctor Jazz – www.doctorjazz.co.uk/page34a.html

Classical Net, Scott Joplin – www.classical.net/music/comp.lst/joplin.php

Encyclopaedia Britannica, Ragtime – www.britannica.com/art/ragtime#ref279958

Encyclopedia.com, Scott Joplin, Composer, Pianist – www.encyclopedia.com/people/literature-and-arts/music-popular-and-jazz-biographies-scott-joplin

Gross, Klaus-Dieter, The Politics of Scott Joplin's "Treemonisha," *Amerikastudien/American Studies*, Vol. 45 No. 3 (2000), Universitatsverlag (WINTER)

Kennethmacmillian.com, Elite Syncopations, 1974 – www.kennethmacmillan.com/elite-syncopations

Library of Congress, Scott Joplin. 1868-1917 – www.loc.gov/item/ihas.200035815

Melton, Larry, Scott Joplin's Treemonisha: The First Stagings Remembered, March 29, 2019, Syncopated

Times – www.syncopatedtimes.com/scott-joplins-treemonisha-the-first-stagings-remembered

Powers, Frank, Wilbur Sweatman, Artist Biography, All Music – www.allmusic.com/artist/wilbur-sweatman-mn0000820923/biography

Scott Joplin, lat.fm, Biography – www.last.fm/music/Scott+Joplin/+wiki

Scott Joplin.org, The Man and His Music – www.scottjoplin.orgt/joplin-biography.html

Reed, Addison W., Scott Joplin, Pioneer, *The Black Perspective in Music*, Vol. 13 No 1 (Spring, 1975)

Reed, Addison W., Scott Joplin: Questions Remain, *Black Music Research Journal.* Vol. 10 No. 1 (Spring, 1990) Columbia College Chicago, University of Illinois Press, Center for Black Music Research

Sedalia Weekly Conservator, Sedalia, MO, Sept. 16, 1904 www.findagrave.com/memorial/82753051/freddie-joplin

US OPERA, Harry Lawrence Freeman – www.usopera.com/composers/freeman.html

Free Books by Charles River Editors

We have brand new titles available for free most days of the week. To see which of our titles are currently free, click on this link.

Discounted Books by Charles River Editors

We have titles at a discount price of just 99 cents everyday. To see which of our titles are currently 99 cents, click on this link.

CPSIA information can be obtained
at www.ICGtesting.com
Printed in the USA
LVHW061618120421
684241LV00009B/806